THE *Map* TO ABUNDANCE WORKBOOK

THE NO-EXCEPTIONS PLANNER FOR CREATING MONEY, SUCCESS, & BLISS

BONI LONNSBURRY

Inner Art, Inc.
1750 30th Street, Suite 543
Boulder, CO 80301

www.innerartinc.com

Editor: Bryna Haynes, www.TheHeartofWriting.com.
Cover & interior design: Bryna Haynes
Interior graphics: Devon Gibbs/Dreamstime stock images

Ordering Information

Quantity sales. Special discounts are available on quantity purchases by corporations, associations, and others. For details, please contact the publisher at the address above.

Publisher's Cataloging-In-Publication Data

Lonnsburry, Boni,

    The Map to Abundance Workbook: The No-Exceptions Guide for Creating Money, Success, & Bliss/ Boni Lonnsburry.
    p. cm.

ISBN13: 978-1-941322-16-1

1. Nonfiction > Self-Help > Personal Growth > Success
2. Nonfiction > Body, Mind & Spirit > New Thought

This workbook is dedicated to our ever-abundant multiverse.

We are all so, so blessed.

TABLE of CONTENTS

INTRODUCTION

How The Map Works

*I*f you've picked up this workbook, you probably have one burning question: "Will this book help me create money?" The answer is, yes it will—and so much more!

As I wrote in my award-winning book, *The Map: To Our Responsive Universe, Where Dreams Really Do Come True!* we are all more powerful than we know. We are literally creating our entire universe twenty-four hours a day, seven days a week. In fact, if you can think and feel, you can consciously create. It's as simple as that.

The Map to Abundance, in combination with this workbook, will help you take your power and ability to the next level—the fully conscious, totally-at-your-fingertips level. This will allow your world to be not only financially sound, but fully abundant in every other area of your life as well.

Being abundant is about far more than having money—although that is a splendid way to begin. Being abundant is about being able to receive all the gifts of this world, and the worlds beyond.

Because of your divine origin, you've been given a priceless gift: the power to single-handedly create abundance in every area of your life. Learning to receive that gift is at the heart of abundance.

So, let's get started, and create even more of the life you came here to live!

In joyous creation,

TWO MORE THINGS TO CONSIDER...

First, if you picked up this workbook in a desperate attempt to keep from drowning financially, please go directly to Appendix A of *The Map to Abundance* and read "In Case of Financial Emergency— Read This!" It will help you calm down and get centered enough to apply the exercises in this workbook thoroughly, and institute permanent change.

Second, I discuss a lot about negative beliefs in this book— because I'd bet anything that your beliefs are a big factor in what stops your abundance. For your convenience in testing for and changing those beliefs, please refer to the instructions in Appendices B, C, and D of *The Map to Abundance*.

THE MAP PROCESS

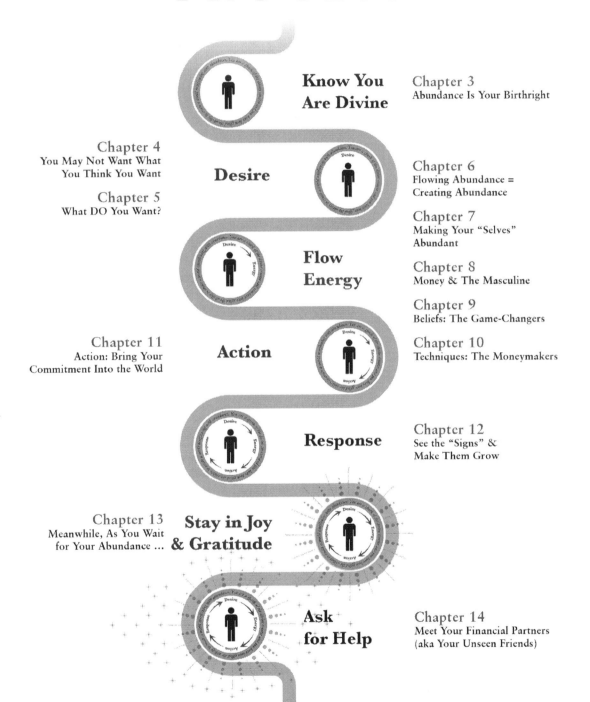

Know You Are Divine

Chapter 3
Abundance Is Your Birthright

Chapter 4
You May Not Want What
You Think You Want

Chapter 5
What DO You Want?

Desire

Chapter 6
Flowing Abundance =
Creating Abundance

Chapter 7
Making Your "Selves"
Abundant

Flow Energy

Chapter 8
Money & The Masculine

Chapter 9
Beliefs: The Game-Changers

Chapter 11
Action: Bring Your
Commitment Into the World

Action

Chapter 10
Techniques: The Moneymakers

Response

Chapter 12
See the "Signs" &
Make Them Grow

Chapter 13
Meanwhile, As You Wait
for Your Abundance ...

Stay in Joy & Gratitude

Ask for Help

Chapter 14
Meet Your Financial Partners
(aka Your Unseen Friends)

CHAPTER ONE

You Never Need to Worry
About Money Again

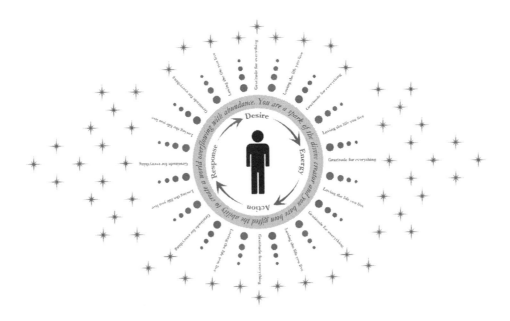

*Y*ou are vastly more powerful than you know. But chances are, your parents didn't teach you this. Nor did your teachers, your friends, or the television. In fact, the knowledge that you create your own reality may be a revelation to you.

Our power to consciously create our reality is quite possibly the world's best-kept secret. I mean, this is epic, right? And yet, few people know about it, and fewer yet manage to actually change their lives with that knowledge.

Why?

Because most people don't really know how it works. Even those who have read the books and attended the seminars struggle with exactly how to create a reality.

The truth is, creating your reality is not hard at all. Actually it's easier than breathing. You already create your reality whether you know it or not, and you do it all the time. We all do. We can't help but create our reality.

It's the way our universe works.

Most people aren't conscious of how they create. They aren't aware of the thoughts, feelings, beliefs, and patterns playing out in the background of their lives. And so, they end up with realities that seem totally unrelated to what they say they want. They're creating unconsciously.

As it pertains to abundance, your unconscious creations usually look like what your parents (or other authority figures) created, or what your parents (or authority figures) expected you to create. Why? Because you unconsciously learn to create unconsciously from other unconscious creators.

Boy, that's a mouthful.

Let me put it another way: **you take on the thoughts, feelings, and beliefs of those around you.** Most particularly, you take on the thoughts, feelings, and beliefs of those you deemed powerful when you were growing up. And, since your thoughts, feelings, and beliefs create your world, if you're not fully aware of what you took on without knowing it, you can end up creating your life in the image of others' lives. It's sort of like watching a remake of an old movie: the actors, scenes, and special effects are different, but the plot is exactly the same.

How do you get off the replay loop? **First, you need to change the way you feel about your reality—both the one you have, and the one you want.**

Abundance Action 1

What was your childhood like regarding money? Write down your early feelings, impressions, and memories about money.

What did your parents or other authority figures say and do when it came to money?

On a scale of 1 to 10, how easy has it been for you to create money or other abundances as an adult?

1   2   3   4   5   6   7   8   9   10

What is the pattern of money flowing into and out of your life?

What have you felt you need to "sacrifice" in order to have money?

On a scale of 1 to 10, how easy is it for you to accept that you are creating 100% of your reality?

1   2   3   4   5   6   7   8   9   10

Why do you think that is?

Abundance Action 2

What are the beliefs you are still carrying about money from your childhood?

MY BELIEFS ABOUT MONEY & ABUNDANCE

1. _____

2. _____

3. _____

4. _____

5. _____

6. _____

7. _____

8. _____

9. _____

10. _____

Hint: You can test for these beliefs using the applied kinesiology techniques in Appendix B of The Map to Abundance!

CHAPTER TWO

The Map to Abundance

Creating an abundant life—a life filled with money, resources, opportunities, freedom, time, joy, health, love, and anything else you want in abundance—is available to you, and to every other sentient being on the planet.

Before you do it, though, it feels like it just won't work—like you're fooling yourself.

But it *does* work—and it *can* work for you.

I have created a ton of abundance in my life—but I wasn't "lucky," or "special," and I didn't end up here by accident. I created this incredible life, my friend—just like you can create your incredible life, if you follow the seven key steps in *The Map to Abundance.*

The Seven Key Steps in *The Map to Abundance*

- **Step 1:** Own Your Power & Divinity

- **Step 2:** Get Clear on What You *Really* Want

- **Step 3:** Flow Energy Toward the Abundance You Seek

- **Step 4:** Take Action to Accelerate Your Creation

- **Step 5:** See the "Signs" & Make them Grow

- **Step 6:** Stay Happy, Grateful, & Feeling "As If"

- **Step 7:** Ask for Help

These steps are described in detail in *The Map to Abundance*. What I want you to dig into here are the qualities you'll need to cultivate to make these steps work.

In order to become a true conscious creator, you must be willing to be:

- Impeccable

- Intimate

- Honest

- Patient

- Relentless

- Open to receive

- Ready to change (for real!)

Abundance Action 1

Are you ready to commit to being ...

IMPECCABLE — What would it look like for you to tackle this journey with everything you have, no excuses, and bring as much of your full self to the table as possible?

INTIMATE — What would it look like for you to embrace the weak, fearful, and shadowed parts of yourself?

HONEST — What would it take for you to experience total transparency with yourself?

PATIENT — Do you consider yourself a patient person? How can you become more patient with yourself so you can take the time you need to heal the past, change your beliefs, and actually create your abundance?

RELENTLESS — Do you give up too easily? What would it look like for you to never give up your efforts to consciously create?

OPEN TO RECEIVE — Are you willing to ask for help from your seen and unseen friends around your creation process? Why or why not?

Want to learn more about your unseen friends? Check out my book, Messages from Your Unseen Friends: Volume I at www.livealifeyoulove.com/messages-from-your-unseen-friends-ebook/

READY TO CHANGE — Are you excited about the "new you," or are you resisting change? What do you love about the new "you" you're creating? What scares you?

Abundance Action 2

It's time to get your Unseen Friends on board!

Below, and on the next page, write about your Unseen Friends. What do you know about them? How do they support you? How can you call on them more often and cultivate greater trust in their support?

{extra writing space}

Feeling stuck about how to communicate with your unseen friends? Clear your mind and ask, "What is the best way for me to hear your wisdom?" Get quiet and trust the answers you receive. You may be surprised at just how close your Unseen Friends already are to you!

CHAPTER THREE

Abundance Is Your Birthright

You are a spark of the divine creator and you have been gifted the ability to create a world overflowing with abundance.

*Y*ou don't create success and abundance because you deserve it. You create success and abundance because you believe you deserve it.

Since many of us weren't taught as children that we're divine, and that we deserve every good thing under the sun, we have to change our beliefs around deservability in order to let those good things in.

Now, the tables have turned, and you are in the driver's seat. You *know* you have a choice, and that your abundance is not outside of your control.

You see, when you believe there's no choice about how you experience your reality, there really is no choice. But when that curtain of possibility has been raised even a sliver, you, my friend, can never go back.

You can never un-know what you now know. And if you're reading this, you're ready to acknowledge that some part of you, the deepest part of you, knows that *you create it all.*

Feeling "undeserving" isn't the only thing that will stop abundance. So will …

- Feeling guilty for having abundance.
- Feeling as if there is only so much to go around and if you have it others won't.
- Feeling as if you don't "do" enough to earn the abundance you desire.
- Feeling like you have to work really hard for abundance.
- Feeling powerless to make money "just happen" in your life.

Truly, the list could go on and on, but you get the picture. Many things will stop you from being abundant, and from allowing money, opportunities, and wealth in all forms to become a permanent part of your reality.

It doesn't matter why you haven't created abundance until now. For whatever reason, you simply weren't ready. But you *are* ready now. Let's begin.

Abundance Action 1

"I am a divine being."

What do these words mean to you? How do they make you feel?

List a few ways you can remind yourself every day that you are a divine being capable of creating and receiving abundance in all its forms.

Ask God and Goddess to help you own the fact of your divine nature more deeply than ever before. Then, go about your day as if you were divine.

Abundance Action 2

Right here, right now, say these words, in your head or aloud:

"I choose to claim my divine right to be abundant. I ask my unseen friends to accompany me on this journey of growth and empowerment and to help me along the way. I ask that you gently point out where I get stuck, show me the beliefs I need to change, and help me to change them. Assist me please, to the greatest extent possible. Thank you in advance for your support, love, guidance, and grace."

Now, in the space below, write a bit about how saying this made you feel. What came up for you as you spoke? What thoughts or feelings rose up to support or challenge your choice to be abundant?

Abundance Action 3

Read aloud and sign the Commitment to Abundance below.

Out of my love for myself and the love I have for my higher self, soul, God, and Goddess, I make these commitments with the intention to live a life of abundance:

- *I commit to remembering the truth: that I am divine by my very nature. I am a part of God and Goddess.*

- *I commit to remembering that my unseen friends love me unconditionally.*

- *I commit to remembering that I live in a reality of my own making—a reality that has the potential to be limitlessly abundant.*

- *I commit to doing the work necessary to free myself to live that unlimitedly abundant life, no matter how difficult and uncomfortable the process may be.*

- *I commit to being totally honest with myself about my limitations, agendas, beliefs, rationalizations, and payoffs.*

- *I commit to forgiving myself for all the times I settled for struggle and hardship, when, looking back, I could have created abundance.*

- *I commit to remembering that abundance is more than money, more than things, more than what "I have." Abundance is who I am becoming: a spiritual being in a physical body who knows beyond a doubt that ease, elegance, resources, magic, synchronicity, love, and guidance are not only my choice, but my birthright.*

- *I commit to asking for and receiving help from my unseen friends, so that they can help me make the journey to a life of abundance as easy, elegant, rich, and fun as possible.*

Signed with abundant love,

_____ Date _____

When you're done, tear out this page and hang it where you will see it often. Or, download a printable version at www.LiveALifeYouLove.com/commitment-abundance.

Abundance Action 4

As you read (or reread) Chapter Three of *The Map to Abundance*, take notes about anything that comes up for you in the space below. Ask yourself, "Why do I feel resistance to this?"

— MY NOTES ON CHAPTER THREE —

CHAPTER FOUR

You May Not Want What
You Think You Want

Money, in and of itself, is useless.

You desire *more* than an abundance of money. You also want an abundance of freedom, health, love, happiness, peace, safety, security, and fun. Without these additional abundances, any money you had would be nearly, if not completely, useless. When you create your intentions around abundance, remember that an abundant life is a life overflowing with abundances of *all* kinds.

Real prosperity and abundance benefit all mankind. Whenever you raise your resonance to create an increase in abundance (or any other good thing) in your life, you're impacting others positively. It can be no other way; this is the way our universe works. What is good for you is good for the world. So be abundant—for yourself, and for others!

Abundance Action 1

What is your biggest, most powerful motivation for creating abundance?

What does this motivation tell you about your beliefs regarding money and abundance?

Abundance Action 2

What beliefs did you uncover about how you "must" create and sustain money in your life?

MY BELIEFS ABOUT HOW AND WHY I CAN
CREATE MONEY & ABUNDANCE IN MY LIFE

1. _____

2. _____

3. _____

4. _____

5. _____

6. _____

7. _____

Hint: You can test for these beliefs using the applied kinesiology techniques in Appendix B of The Map to Abundance!

NOTE: If any of these beliefs are not supporting you, change them as soon as possible using one of the tools in Appendix D of *The Map to Abundance.*

{extra writing space}

CHAPTER FIVE

What *Do* You Want?

Now we get to the exciting part—dreaming your juicy, fulfilling, succulent future of abundance!

As I've mentioned before, no dream about abundance is inherently wrong. No matter what you want, you *can* have it. The universe always says "yes."

But, here's the catch: just because it's *possible* to create something doesn't mean you *will* create it.

I want to make you aware of what is going on beneath the surface of your dreams in order to heal and change any energy that may be sabotaging them. I also intend to help you get clear on what it is you truly desire—because *true desires are always creatable.*

Abundance Action 1

On a scale of 1 to 10, with regard to abundance of money, love, fulfillment, joy, and other good things in your life, where are you currently?

MONEY   1 2 3 4 5 6 7 8 9 10

JOY   1 2 3 4 5 6 7 8 9 10

FULFILLMENT   1 2 3 4 5 6 7 8 9 10

RELATIONSHIPS 1 2 3 4 5 6 7 8 9 10

WORK/CAREER   1 2 3 4 5 6 7 8 9 10

HEALTH   1 2 3 4 5 6 7 8 9 10

FUN   1 2 3 4 5 6 7 8 9 10

Abundance Action 2

Using one of the testing techniques in Appendix B of *The Map to Abundance,* test for the following limiting beliefs:

BELIEF	TRUE FOR ME (Y/N)?
I DON'T DESERVE TO BE RICH.	Y N
I DON'T DESERVE TO BE ABUNDANT.	Y N
I AM NOT GOOD ENOUGH TO BE WEALTHY.	Y N
MONEY IN THIS WORLD IS LIMITED.	Y N
IF I CREATE MORE MONEY FOR MYSELF, SOMEONE WILL GO WITHOUT.	Y N
IT IS WRONG TO DESIRE MONEY.	Y N
MONEY IS BAD.	Y N
SPIRITUAL PEOPLE DO NOT DESIRE MONEY.	Y N
GOOD PEOPLE DO NOT SEEK TO BE WEALTHY.	Y N

Which (if any) of these beliefs are true for you? What was your reaction to learning that you carried these beliefs?

Abundance Action 3

Using one of the testing techniques in Appendix B of *The Map to Abundance*, **test for the following additional limiting beliefs:**

BELIEF	TRUE FOR ME (Y/N)?
I CAN'T TRUST MONEY TO COME IN EXACTLY WHEN I NEED OR WANT IT.	Y N
I CAN'T TRUST MYSELF TO CREATE MONEY WHEN I NEED OR WANT IT.	Y N
I HAVE TO BE UBER-PREPARED IN CASE OF EMERGENCY.	Y N
JUST WHEN SOME THINGS GO RIGHT, THE OTHER SHOE WILL DROP.	Y N
I MAY BE ABLE TO MANIFEST MONEY SOMETIMES, BUT NOT ALL THE TIME.	Y N
I AM NOT WORTHY.	Y N
MY WORTH IS BASED ON WHAT I HAVE, NOT ON WHO I AM.	Y N
I AM NOT VALUABLE.	Y N
I AM A FAILURE.	Y N
I AM A DISAPPOINTMENT.	Y N

If you have any of the above beliefs (or any of the beliefs from Abundance Action 2), change them as soon as possible using one of the tools in Appendix D of The Map to Abundance.

Abundance Action 4

Did any other limiting beliefs surface for you while you were reading Chapter Five? If so, write them here and change them as soon as possible.

MY BELIEFS

1. _____

2. _____

3. _____

4. _____

5. _____

6. _____

7. _____

Abundance Action 5

Using the prompts below, write your intentions for becoming a stellar conscious creator, and for all forms of abundance.

• • ● MY OVERALL INTENTION ● • •

• • ● MY CORE INTENTIONS ● • •

My intention for money:

My intention for work:

My intention for health:

My intention for relationships:

My intention for fun:

My intention for learning and growth:

• • ● MY IMMEDIATE INTENTIONS ●● •

List the specific things you desire right now. Be sure to include the emotional states you want to feel when these things manifest!

● Immediate intention #1:

● Immediate intention #2:

● Immediate intention #3:

● Immediate intention #4:

● Immediate intention #5:

Abundance Action 6

How will you work with your intentions? Write down a few ideas for how you can work with your intentions every day. For example, you could:

- Post them around your house so you will see them often.
- Read them aloud every morning.
- Create a piece of art or a vision board that captures their essence.

{extra writing space}

CHAPTER SIX

Flowing Abundance = Creating Abundance

Desire

Energy

...abundance. You are a spark of the divine creator and you have been gifted the ability to create a world overflowing with...

Most of us aren't patient enough to allow abundance to manifest according to the universe's timing. This impatience pushes your dream further away, which creates feelings of lack, despair, and frustration.

And, even when we master the art of patience, we may be unconsciously flowing other energies that oppose our dream. This opposing flow slows things down, or even stops them from manifesting altogether.

The energy you put forth attracts realities that match your energy. That's why, in this chapter, we'll target your "Abundance Stoppers"—feelings of lack, scarcity, and struggle that get in the way of you manifesting the abundance you desire.

Abundance Action 1

Do you have doubts about your ability to create abundance? What beliefs keep them alive? Write about this below, then list any associated beliefs so you can change them.

BELIEFS TO CHANGE

1. _____

2. _____

3. _____

Abundance Action 2

What fearful scenarios about money and abundance do you replay in your head? What beliefs do they point to? Write about this below, then list any associated beliefs so you can change them.

BELIEFS TO CHANGE

1. _____

2. _____

3. _____

Abundance Action 3

What doubts do you have about creating an abundant life? What fears (and beliefs) underpin those doubts? Write about this below.

BELIEFS TO CHANGE

1. _____

2. _____

3. _____

Abundance Action 4

Do you have a propensity to feel hopeless, helpless, powerless, and/or that life isn't fair? Do you complain to your friends and family? Do you tend to worry more than not? Write about this below. Include any beliefs that are keeping your victimhood locked in place.

BELIEFS TO CHANGE

1. _____

2. _____

3. _____

Abundance Action 5

Do you feel a sense of entitlement to receive anything in your life? If so, process the constricting emotions, then look for the beliefs that keep your entitlement from being released.

BELIEFS TO CHANGE

1. _____

2. _____

3. _____

Abundance Action 6

What do your relationships say about your abundance?

Do you greatly admire anyone you know? What does that person being in your life tell you about yourself and your ability to create?

Do you feel envious of anyone you know? What beliefs does that envy reveal?

Abundance Action 7

On a scale of 1-10, how deserving do you feel?

1   2   3   4   5   6   7   8   9   10

Do you have any beliefs regarding your deservability that you would like to change?

BELIEFS TO CHANGE

1. _____

2. _____

3. _____

Abundance Action 8

Does guilt come up for you when you think about creating and having abundance? If so, write about it below. Then, follow the strategies outlined in Chapter Six of *The Map to Abundance* to deactivate it.

Abundance Action 9

Use the applied kinesiology techniques in Appendix B to test for the constricting beliefs discussed throughout Chapter Six of *The Map to Abundance*. Document the beliefs that need to be changed, and change them using a technique in Appendix D.

BELIEFS TO CHANGE

1. _____

2. _____

3. _____

4. _____

5. _____

6. _____

7. _____

8. _____

9. _____

10. _____

Abundance Action 10

Write a letter to your unseen friends. Ask them to help you get clear on any abundance stoppers that are showing up in your life, and help you heal and change the habit.

Dear _____,

HINT: You can write to all of your unseen friends, or just one (God, Goddess, future self, higher self, soul, etc.). What's important is that you're asking for help!

With Love and Gratitude,

_____
(your signature)

{extra writing space}

CHAPTER SEVEN

Making Your "Selves" Abundant

Desire — *Energy*

You are a spark of the divine creator and you have been gifted the ability to create a world overflowing with abundance.

$\mathcal{Y}$ou're not a blank slate when it comes to money. You've been programmed to truly believe that it is beyond your ability to create money out of thin air. You probably also have a slew of failures in your back pocket that prove you can't create it by hard work and desire alone, either.

You can't fix a conundrum like your programmed beliefs and experiences around money with the same thinking that created it. You have to step outside the box, and do things in a new way—the *right* way.

In other words, you need to step into *alignment* with abundance on all levels, across all of your various "selves."

Abundance Action 1

Before you're free to create abundance, you need to forgive yourself for not creating abundance in the past. What less-than-stellar realities do you need to forgive yourself for creating? What realities of scarcity and lack? What hurts or betrayals? Remember: Everything is forgivable.

Abundance Action 2

Write out what you intend to forgive yourself for in the space below. Sign it three times.

Signed,

_____

_____

_____

(This exercise is continued on the next page.)

In a meditation, meet the person you intend to forgive or ask forgiveness from. (Note: This person might be a younger aspect of you.) Meet them at night, around a bonfire of forgiveness. Talk to them. Ask for their forgiveness.

Write about your experience below. When you're finished, tear out this page and burn it in meditation. Feel the freedom of forgiveness!

• • ● MY FORGIVENESS MEDITATION ● • •

Abundance Action 3

Visit your child self in meditation. Talk to them about creating abundance. Listen to what they have to say, and witness what they allow themselves to feel. When they are complete, give them a money machine and watch their response.

When you come out of meditation, write down what they said in the space below, and determine the beliefs underlying those statements. Write those down as well.

BELIEFS TO CHANGE

1. _____

2. _____

3. _____

Abundance Action 4

Visit your adolescent self in meditation. Talk to them about creating abundance. Listen to what they have to say, and witness what they allow themselves to feel. When they are complete, give them a money machine and watch their response.

When you come out of meditation, write down what they said in the space below, and determine the beliefs underlying those statements. Write those down as well.

BELIEFS TO CHANGE

1. _____

2. _____

3. _____

Abundance Action 5

Make a list of the major financial and career disappointments of your life. When you're done, one by one, visit with these disappointed selves. Let them vent, cry, complain, and get angry. Allow them free reign of emotion. When they're complete, give them what they wanted at the time, even if it's something you no longer desire. Watch them for a while—happy as can be in the reality they dreamed of.

• • ● MY BIGGEST FINANCIAL/CAREER ● • • DISAPPOINTMENTS

● Big Disappointment #1:

● Big Disappointment #2:

● Big Disappointment #3:

(This exercise is continued on the next page.)

- Big Disappointment #4:

- Big Disappointment #5:

••● MEDITATIVE EXPERIENCES ●••

Abundance Action 6

Imagine your "negative self" sitting next to you. Tell it that you're learning how to create unlimited abundance. In the space below, write down everything it has to say.

• ● ●   NEGATIVE SELF'S RANT   ● ● •

When you're done with this exercise, call in your higher self to take your negative self away to be healed; then, if you like, tear out and (safely) burn this page.

Abundance Action 7

Use the applied kinesiology techniques in Appendix B to test for the constricting beliefs discussed throughout Chapter Seven of *The Map to Abundance*. Document the beliefs that need to be changed, and change them using a technique in Appendix D.

BELIEFS TO CHANGE

1. _____

2. _____

3. _____

4. _____

5. _____

6. _____

7. _____

8. _____

9. _____

10. _____

CHAPTER EIGHT

Money & The Masculine

Money is a "masculine" energy.

I know that sounds more than a little woo-woo, but bear with me. Ultimately, it doesn't matter if money is masculine, feminine, or androgynous—what matters is your *emotional relationship* with money.

If you fear money, fear having money, fear being judged because you have money, or fear someone will take your money away once you have it, then you won't create it. And, since this book is dedicated to looking under every possible emotional rock to make sure nothing is lurking there which will sabotage your abundance, we are going to delve into your energetic relationship with the masculine nature of money.

Abundance Action 1

In the past, did you feel loved, cherished, and supported by the following? Why or why not? What experiences stand out?

Your father:

Other authority figures (teachers, bosses, mentors, etc.):

God:

Abundance Action 2

If, in the past, you didn't feel supported by your father, other authority figures, or God, use the exercise in Chapter Eight to go back and visit with your younger selves. Let them express their sorrow, frustration, and hurt. Write about the experience below.

Abundance Action 3

Do you feel that tithing (or giving financially in some way), is required of you when you allow your abundance? Why or why not?

What underlying beliefs do you want to change with regard to this?

BELIEFS TO CHANGE

1. _____

2. _____

3. _____

Abundance Action 4

Use the applied kinesiology techniques in Appendix B to test for the constricting beliefs discussed throughout Chapter Eight of *The Map to Abundance*. Document the beliefs that need to be changed, and change them using a technique in Appendix D.

BELIEFS TO CHANGE

1. _____

2. _____

3. _____

4. _____

5. _____

6. _____

7. _____

8. _____

9. _____

10. _____

{extra writing space}

CHAPTER NINE

Beliefs: The Game-Changers

The beliefs we learn as children are the building blocks of our creations as adults. However …

It's not actually what you experience that forms your beliefs. It's what you decide about that experience.

Your beliefs rule your reality. I don't know how to say it stronger than that. Your beliefs are keeping you where you are—not your past choices, not your family history, not your environment, and not the world at large.

If you believe in struggle, *you will struggle.* If you believe money is tough to come by, *it will be tough to come by.* If you believe you are powerless to change your "luck," *you will be powerless.*

Your past does not have to dictate your future—but it probably will, unless you change the unhelpful beliefs stored in your subconscious mind.

Abundance Action 1

Use the applied kinesiology techniques in Appendix B to test for the following constricting beliefs. Test ten beliefs at a time, with a five-minute break between sets.

FOUNDATIONAL BELIEFS

BELIEF	TRUE FOR ME (Y/N)?
IT IS IMPOSSIBLE TO CREATE MY OWN REALITY.	Y N

It is not possible/easy:

WE DON'T REALLY CREATE OUR OWN REALITIES.	Y N
I CAN'T CREATE MY REALITY.	Y N
I CAN'T CHANGE MY BELIEFS.	Y N
IT IS DIFFICULT TO CREATE MY REALITY.	Y N
IT IS HARD TO CHANGE BELIEFS.	Y N
I CAN'T EASILY DISCOVER MY SUBCONSCIOUS BELIEFS.	Y N
I CAN'T CHANGE MY BELIEFS ABOUT _____ [MONEY, LOVE, MEN, WOMEN, HEALTH, WORK, ETC.].	Y N

It works for everyone else but me:

EVEN IF I "CHANGE MY BELIEFS," MY WORLD WILL NOT CHANGE.	Y N
NOTHING EVER WORKS FOR ME.	Y N
I DON'T HAVE WHAT IT TAKES TO CHANGE MY BELIEFS, AND THUS MY LIFE.	Y N

BELIEF	TRUE FOR ME (Y/N)?
I DON'T HAVE THE POWER OR ABILITY TO CREATE MY WORLD.	Y N
IT IS HARD TO CREATE WHAT I WANT.	Y N
I AM NOT POWERFUL ENOUGH TO CHANGE MY BELIEFS.	Y N

It is wrong/unspiritual to create my reality:

IT IS WRONG TO CHANGE MY BELIEFS.	Y N
I'LL BE PUNISHED IF I CHANGE MY BELIEFS.	Y N
ONLY GOD CAN CHANGE MY BELIEFS.	Y N
IT IS UNSPIRITUAL TO CHANGE MY BELIEFS.	Y N
ONLY GOD CAN CREATE MY REALITY.	Y N
IT IS BLASPHEMOUS TO BELIEVE I CAN CREATE MY OWN REALITY.	Y N

I'm not ready:

I'M NOT READY TO CHANGE MY BELIEFS ABOUT _____ [MONEY, LOVE, MEN, HEALTH, WORK, ETC.].	Y N
I'M NOT READY FOR THE SUCCESS THAT WILL HAPPEN WHEN I CHANGE MY BELIEFS.	Y N
I CAN HAVE THE REALITIES I DESIRE ONLY AFTER I CLEAR OUT ALL MY BLOCKAGES.	Y N
I'M NOT HEALED ENOUGH TO CREATE MY REALITY.	Y N
IF I SUCCESSFULLY CREATE MY OWN REALITY, THE RESPONSIBILITY OF MAINTAINING IT WOULD BE TOO MUCH FOR ME TO HANDLE.	Y N
I'M NOT _____ [OLD, YOUNG, WISE, CAPABLE, SEASONED, EXPERIENCED, SMART, ETC.] ENOUGH TO CREATE MY OWN REALITY.	Y N

BELIEF	TRUE FOR ME (Y/N)?

It's not safe:

MY SUCCESS THAT HAPPENS AS A RESULT OF CHANGING MY BELIEFS WILL MAKE PEOPLE I CARE ABOUT FEEL BADLY ABOUT THEIR OWN LIVES.	Y N
IF I CHANGE MY BELIEFS ABOUT _____ [MONEY, LOVE, MEN, HEALTH, WORK, OTHER PEOPLE, ETC.] AND MY WORLD CHANGES, SOMEONE I CARE ABOUT WILL BE HURT.	Y N
SOMETHING BAD WILL HAPPEN IF I CHANGE MY BELIEFS.	Y N
IT'S NOT SAFE TO CREATE ALL THAT I WANT.	Y N
IF I BELIEVE IN THIS INFORMATION OTHERS WILL RIDICULE ME.	Y N

BELIEFS ABOUT MONEY

Beliefs about the value of money:

MONEY IS THE ROOT OF ALL EVIL.	Y N
MONEY IS DIRTY.	Y N
MONEY IS A CURSE.	Y N
MONEY IS POWER.	Y N
MONEY IS FREEDOM.	Y N
MONEY IS EVERYTHING.	Y N
MONEY MEASURES WORTH.	Y N
MONEY MAKES YOU DESIRABLE TO OTHERS.	Y N
MONEY MAKES YOU HAPPY.	Y N
RICH PEOPLE ARE BETTER THAN POOR PEOPLE.	Y N
POOR PEOPLE ARE BETTER THAN RICH PEOPLE.	Y N

BELIEF	**TRUE FOR ME (Y/N)?**

Beliefs about you and money:

I DON'T DESERVE A LOT OF MONEY.	Y N
MY SPOUSE/PARTNER CREATES MONEY BUT I DON'T.	Y N
I CAN'T HANDLE HAVING MONEY.	Y N
I CAN'T HAVE MONEY.	Y N
I CAN'T SAVE MONEY.	Y N
I AM ALWAYS IN DEBT.	Y N
I DON'T HAVE ENOUGH MONEY TO SHARE OR GIVE AWAY.	Y N
I AM SMART AND TALENTED, THEREFORE I SHOULD GET MORE MONEY.	Y N
I WORK SUPER HARD, I DESERVE MORE MONEY.	Y N
I DON'T KNOW HOW TO MAKE MONEY.	Y N
I DON'T KNOW HOW TO CREATE MONEY.	Y N
I CAN NEVER GET AHEAD.	Y N
I HATE MONEY.	Y N
I AM A FAILURE WHEN IT COMES TO MONEY.	Y N
I WOULD FEEL GUILTY IF I HAD MORE MONEY THAN [NAME].	Y N
OTHERS CAN CREATE MONEY BUT NOT ME.	Y N
THE ECONOMY IS RESPONSIBLE FOR MY MONEY PROBLEMS.	Y N
[NAME, ENTITY, EVENT] IS RESPONSIBLE FOR MY MONEY PROBLEMS.	Y N
IF I DON'T WORRY ABOUT MONEY SOMETHING BAD WILL HAPPEN.	Y N

BELIEF	TRUE FOR ME (Y/N)?

Beliefs about the ease with which money comes to you:

YOU HAVE TO EARN THE MONEY YOU MAKE.	Y N
MONEY COMES WITH INCREDIBLE STRUGGLE.	Y N
MAKING MONEY TAKES A LOT OF HARD WORK.	Y N
IT TAKES MONEY TO MAKE MONEY.	Y N
THERE IS NEVER ENOUGH MONEY.	Y N
THERE IS ALWAYS JUST ENOUGH MONEY.	Y N
THERE IS NEVER MORE THAN ENOUGH MONEY.	Y N
MONEY IS HARD TO COME BY.	Y N
I NEED TO EARN MY MONEY.	Y N
THERE IS NOT ENOUGH MONEY TO GO AROUND.	Y N
THE UNIVERSE IS LIMITED IN ITS ABUNDANCE.	Y N
MONEY ONLY COMES TO ME THROUGH MY JOB.	Y N
ONLY A SELECT FEW GET TO HAVE MONEY.	Y N
IF A LOT OF MONEY COMES EASILY, IT MUST BE ILLEGAL.	Y N
YOU NEED TO BE SUPER SMART TO MAKE A LOT OF MONEY.	Y N

Beliefs about what you have to give up to get money:

IF I AM FINANCIALLY ABUNDANT, I WILL HAVE TO SACRIFICE MY HAPPINESS.	Y N
IF I AM FINANCIALLY ABUNDANT, I WILL HAVE TO SACRIFICE MY FAMILY.	Y N
IF I AM FINANCIALLY ABUNDANT, I WILL HAVE TO SACRIFICE MY FREEDOM.	Y N
IF I AM FINANCIALLY ABUNDANT, I WILL HAVE TO SACRIFICE MY INTEGRITY.	Y N
IF I REALLY LIVE MY TRUTH, I'LL END UP BROKE.	Y N

BELIEF	TRUE FOR ME (Y/N)?

IN ORDER TO BE RICH, YOU MUST SACRIFICE
YOUR FREE TIME.   Y N

YOU CAN'T HAVE MONEY AND HAPPINESS.   Y N

I WILL HAVE TO DO WHAT I HATE IN ORDER
TO HAVE MONEY.   Y N

MONEY WILL CHANGE ME FOR THE WORSE.   Y N

YOU HAVE TO DO LOTS OF THINGS YOU DON'T
LIKE IN ORDER TO HAVE MONEY.   Y N

MONEY ALWAYS COMES WITH STRINGS ATTACHED.   Y N

IT TAKES MONEY TO MAKE MONEY.   Y N

Beliefs about what it means when you have (or don't have) money:

IF A LOT OF MONEY COMES EASILY, IT MUST BE ILLEGAL.   Y N

BEING RICH IS A SIN.   Y N

HAVING MONEY IS GREEDY.   Y N

WANTING MORE MONEY IS SELFISH.   Y N

MONEY SPOILS YOU.   Y N

RICH PEOPLE ARE SNOBS.   Y N

RICH PEOPLE ARE EGOTISTICAL.   Y N

RICH PEOPLE ARE SELFISH.   Y N

RICH PEOPLE ARE EVIL.   Y N

RICH PEOPLE ARE CORRUPT.   Y N

RICH PEOPLE BECOME WEALTHY BY TAKING
ADVANTAGE OF OTHERS.   Y N

THERE IS NOBILITY IN BEING POOR.   Y N

MONEY EQUALS POWER, AND POWER CORRUPTS.   Y N

IF YOU DON'T HAVE MONEY, YOU'RE POWERLESS.   Y N

BELIEF	TRUE FOR ME (Y/N)?

Beliefs about what you have to do to keep money:

I MUST BE SUPER CONSCIOUS OF EVERY SINGLE DOLLAR TO BE SURE I DON'T LOSE THE MONEY I CREATE.	Y N
I MUST SACRIFICE TO SAVE MY MONEY.	Y N
IF I AM NOT HYPER-VIGILANT SOMEONE WILL TAKE MY MONEY.	Y N
I MUST HIDE THE MONEY I CREATE.	Y N

Beliefs about what happens when you get money:

ACCEPTING MONEY OBLIGATES ME.	Y N
WHEN I AM RICH, I WON'T HAVE TIME FOR MY SPIRITUALITY.	Y N
WHEN I AM RICH, I WON'T HAVE TIME FOR MY FRIENDS.	Y N
WHEN I AM RICH, I WON'T HAVE TIME FOR MY FAMILY.	Y N
WHEN I AM RICH, I WILL BE TIED TO OBLIGATIONS AND STRESSED OUT.	Y N
WHEN I AM RICH, I WON'T BE ABLE TO HANDLE THE RESPONSIBILITY.	Y N
PEOPLE WILL LOVE ME ONLY FOR MY MONEY.	Y N
PEOPLE WILL SCORN ME BECAUSE I HAVE MONEY.	Y N
MONEY COMES WITH A LOT OF RESPONSIBILITY.	Y N
PEOPLE ARE MEAN TO RICH PEOPLE.	Y N
IF I HAVE MONEY, I'LL JUST LOSE IT ANYWAY.	Y N
IF I HAVE MONEY, I'LL LOSE ALL MY FRIENDS.	Y N
IF I HAVE MONEY, PEOPLE WILL BE AFTER ME FOR MY MONEY.	Y N
IF I HAVE MONEY, PEOPLE WILL BE JEALOUS OF ME.	Y N

BELIEF	TRUE FOR ME (Y/N)?

IF I HAVE MONEY, PEOPLE WILL JUST WANT ME
FOR MY MONEY.   Y N

IF I HAVE MONEY, OTHERS WILL GO WITHOUT.   Y N

IF I HAVE MONEY, I'LL BE MORE VISIBLE.   Y N

IF I HAVE MONEY, I'LL BE HELD TO PUBLIC SCRUTINY.   Y N

BELIEFS ABOUT SUCCESS & WORK

Beliefs about whether and how success comes to you:

I CAN'T HANDLE SUCCESS.   Y N

OTHERS ARE RESPONSIBLE FOR MY SUCCESS.   Y N

IF I AM SUCCESSFUL, PEOPLE WILL HATE ME.   Y N

SUCCESS IS DIFFICULT.   Y N

I CAN'T BE SUCCESSFUL AND TRUE TO
MYSELF AT THE SAME TIME.   Y N

Beliefs about what happens when you're successful:

IF I AM TOO SUCCESSFUL, SOMEONE WILL TAKE IT AWAY.   Y N

IF I AM TOO VISIBLE, SOMEONE WILL MAKE ME PAY.   Y N

IF I AM SUCCESSFUL, PEOPLE WILL HATE ME.   Y N

IF I AM SUCCESSFUL, I WON'T BE ABLE TO KEEP IT UP.   Y N

I CAN'T HANDLE SUCCESS.   Y N

Beliefs about work:

I CAN'T MAKE THE KIND OF MONEY I WANT BY
DOING SOMETHING THAT FILLS ME WITH JOY.   Y N

BELIEF	TRUE FOR ME (Y/N)?
I CAN'T MAKE ENOUGH MONEY DOING WHAT I TRULY LOVE.	Y N
IT'S A DOG-EAT-DOG WORLD OUT THERE.	Y N
MOST ENTREPRENEURS FAIL, THEREFORE THE ODDS ARE STACKED AGAINST ME.	Y N
IN ORDER TO HAVE THE WORK I DESIRE, I HAVE TO GIVE UP SOME THINGS I VALUE.	Y N
I DON'T KNOW WHAT MY PASSION IS.	Y N

When you're done testing all of the beliefs in this exercise, change them using a technique in Appendix D of *The Map to Abundance*.

• • ● MEDITATIVE EXPERIENCES ● • •

Abundance Action 2

Use the applied kinesiology techniques in Appendix B to test for the following constricting beliefs. Test ten beliefs at a time, with a five-minute break between sets.

CORE BELIEFS *(Note: this list is non-exclusive.)*

<u>BELIEF</u>	<u>TRUE FOR ME (Y/N)?</u>
I AM NOT GOOD ENOUGH.	Y N
I AM FLAWED.	Y N
I AM UNWORTHY.	Y N
I AM NO GOOD.	Y N
I AM UNSUCCESSFUL.	Y N
I AM NOT VALUABLE.	Y N
I AM INFERIOR.	Y N
I AM NOTHING.	Y N
I AM INVISIBLE.	Y N
I AM INSIGNIFICANT.	Y N
I AM UNLOVABLE.	Y N
I AM UNACCEPTABLE.	Y N
I DON'T MATTER.	Y N
I AM UNIMPORTANT.	Y N
I AM A MISTAKE.	Y N
I DON'T BELONG.	Y N
I AM UNWANTED.	Y N
I AM UNWELCOME.	Y N
I DON'T FIT IN ANYWHERE.	Y N
I AM UNBALANCED.	Y N
I AM A FAILURE.	Y N
I DON'T DESERVE.	Y N
I AM A LOSER.	Y N
I AM INADEQUATE.	Y N

Abundance Action 3

Did you test positive for one of the core beliefs in Abundance Action 2? If so, change it using the following process for changing a Level Three (core) belief. (This process is also outlined in Appendix D of *The Map to Abundance*.)

HOW TO CHANGE A LEVEL THREE BELIEF

Preparation

Be specific and really think about how this belief has affected you for your entire life. Write a few paragraphs about this.

Now, write a paragraph about why you don't want to change this belief. (Yes, there is a part of you that doesn't want to change the belief.) Think about this. What are you afraid of? What could go wrong?

Next, check in with your child, adolescent, and young adult selves. What do they need to be okay with you changing this belief? Talk to them individually. Explain to them why you want to change it. Ask them what it would take for them to give you the okay—and whatever it is, give it to them. (Return to Chapter Seven of *The Map to Abundance*, if necessary, to review this technique.)

When you're done, write about your experience below.

Next, write out how your life will change once you have adopted the new belief.

Finally, consider how your self-concept will change with the new belief, and write a paragraph about this.

Changing a Level Three Belief In Your Subconscious Mind

You are now ready to change your core belief. Write out or print out the old and the new beliefs. Then, get into a quiet space, and close your eyes, and begin the meditation below.

LEVEL THREE BELIEF-CHANGING MEDITATION*

Call upon your unseen friends (it doesn't matter if you don't know who they are) to assist you. You can say something like:

> *I call on my angels, higher self, guides, and others who desire to help me successfully change these beliefs. Gently guide, protect, and assist me please, with harm to none.*

Imagine you are in a beautiful place in nature. This place is serene, quiet, and safe. Then imagine your unseen friends coming to be with you, surrounding you in a bubble of love and light. Take a few moments to close your mental eyes and feel the wonderful love and light. Feel the love, guidance, and protection of your unseen friends. When you open your mental eyes you are surrounded in mist. And before you is a grand marble staircase. You, and your unseen friends, begin to walk up this staircase … up, up, up into the clouds.

At the very top of this staircase, you will be at the entrance to a city, which represents your subconscious mind. It could be modern or ancient. It could be a city in nature, with natural caves and carvings in the rocks. It could look like anything at all. It may change shape. Whatever it looks like it is perfect for you.

The king or queen of this city (your subconscious) will soon come to welcome you. Tell them you want to change your beliefs. They will look to your higher self for permission, and your higher self will nod its consent. "Are you *sure?*" they will ask. Your higher self will look at you, and back at the king/queen and say, "Yes, it is time."

Follow the king or queen to the Building of Beliefs. Your higher self will join you. They will take you to the room that holds your Level Three beliefs. They press a secret button—you cannot tell exactly how—and an entire section of cabinets opens up to reveal a secret door.

Purchase this technique as a meditation at www.LiveALifeYouLove.com!

The king/queen goes through the doorway and beckons you to follow. You and your higher self do follow, but you barely catch a glimpse of them as they head down a hallway, and then turn a corner. They twist through long passageways, this way and that. Finally they enter an elevator and you follow, barely making it in before the doors close. The elevator goes up, over, down, then down, over and up … over and over. You have entirely lost track of where you are. The doors open, and the king/queen leads you to a door marked, "Core Beliefs: Do Not Enter."

They unlock the door and allow you to enter. It is a small room. A table sits in the middle of it and on the table is a thin book marked, "My Core Beliefs."

"Now," the king/queen says, "Tell me the belief you want to change."

Tell them the belief you want to change. They will open the book to exactly that belief.

Picking up the thick black marker, you cross out the belief obliterating every word. You rip the page neatly out of the book and tear it into tiny shreds. Your higher self looks at you and asks, "Are you certain? This will change everything." You nod your head. And your higher self points its finger and the belief bursts into flames, leaving nothing behind.

You look down at a clean white page in the book, pick up a thin black marker and begin to write your new belief, saying each and every letter in your mind as you write.

You put down the marker and close the book.

Your higher self and your subconscious mind are grinning. You grin back, thanking them with your eyes. You say your goodbyes, close your mental eyes, and allow yourself to be back where you started … but you are different.

Now, open your eyes.

CONSCIOUS MIND FOLLOW-UP: Write or type out the new belief. Every day, for ninety days, read the new belief twice a day, with as much excitement and joy as you can muster. (If you skip a day, just add another day at the end.

CHAPTER TEN

Techniques: The Moneymakers

*A*bundance is a resonance. And as you follow *The Map to Abundance,* it will help you to create a resonance of abundance that will make techniques unnecessary.

Ultimately you will simply be abundant, and everything will flow to you in perfect timing. You will dance through life joyfully, expecting that all of your needs will be met.

While you're working on your resonance of abundance, these techniques will help you move toward that abundant state of being, and also help you create the specific things you desire. As you work with these techniques, start with smaller dreams, and build up to bigger dreams. Your dreams have to be believable (to you) before they can materialize.

Most of all, have fun with this!

Abundance Action 1

Imagine yourself being surprised by unexpected abundance.
Imagine a picture of yourself smiling, remembering you made this
happen. Do the One-Minute Manifestor Technique twice a day for
seven days with this picture in mind. Write down your observations,
signs, and results for each day below.

THE ONE-MINUTE MANIFESTOR TECHNIQUE*

Preparation

Choose something you want to manifest. You don't need to know the
specifics of how it will come to be, only how you'll feel when you get it.

Then, imagine the scene when you realize that this "dream" has fully
manifested. Obviously you're smiling, maybe even laughing. Perhaps you're
on the phone, calling someone to tell him or her about it. Maybe you're
holding something which symbolizes this dream—like a paycheck, a letter,
or an engagement ring.

Fix this picture in your mind, as if looking at a photograph of yourself.
Realize that the you in the picture feels so joyous because this dream has
just become real in your life.

The Technique

Set a timer for twenty-three seconds. At the very start of those twenty-three
seconds, close your eyes and visualize that joyous picture of yourself. Feel
that joy, that excitement, that unadulterated happiness. Know that you have
your dream.

Hold that picture, and that "over the top" emotion, until the timer goes off
at exactly twenty-three seconds. Then, quickly open your eyes.

Take two deep breaths, reset your timer, and repeat.

Purchase this technique as a meditation at www.LiveALifeYouLove.com!

• •● MY OBSERVATIONS ●● •

● **Day 1**

Abundance picture _____

_____

Signs? (over the following 3 days) Y   N

- _____

- _____

- _____

Other Observations? _____

_____

_____

_____

_____

● **Day 2**

Abundance picture _____

_____

Signs? (over the following 3 days) Y   N

- _____

- _____

- _____

Other Observations? _____

_____

_____

_____

_____

● Day 3

Abundance picture _____

_____

Signs? (over the following 3 days) Y   N

- _____

- _____

- _____

Other Observations? _____

_____

_____

_____

_____

● Day 4

Abundance picture _____

_____

Signs? (over the following 3 days) Y   N

- _____

- _____

- _____

Other Observations? _____

_____

_____

_____

_____

● **Day 5**

Abundance picture _____

_____

Signs? (over the following 3 days) Y   N

•   _____

•   _____

•   _____

Other Observations? _____

_____

_____

_____

_____

● **Day 6**

Abundance picture _____

_____

Signs? (over the following 3 days) Y   N

•   _____

•   _____

•   _____

Other Observations? _____

_____

_____

_____

_____

● **Day 7**

Abundance picture _____
_____

Signs? (over the following 3 days) Y   N

• _____

• _____

• _____

Other Observations? _____
_____
_____
_____
_____

● ● ●   MY OVERALL RESULTS   ● ● ●

Abundance Action 2

THE "YOUR ABUNDANT FUTURE SELF"
TECHNIQUE

Do the Your Abundant Future Self technique described in Chapter Ten of *The Map to Abundance.* Then, write about your experience using the prompts below.

How did you feel before the technique?

How did you feel afterward?

What changes did you see in your reality as a result of the technique?

Abundance Action 3

THE "HOUSE OF ABUNDANCE" TECHNIQUE

Do the House of Abundance technique described in Chapter Ten of *The Map to Abundance*. Then, write about your experience using the prompts below.

How did you feel before the technique?

How did you feel afterward?

What changes did you see in your reality as a result of the technique?

Abundance Action 4

THE "I CAN AFFORD EVERYTHING HERE" TECHNIQUE

Do the I Can Afford Everything Here technique described in Chapter Ten of *The Map to Abundance.* Then, write about your experience using the prompts below.

How did you feel before the technique?

How did you feel afterward?

What changes did you see in your reality as a result of the technique?

Abundance Action 5

THE "ABUNDANCE RITUAL" TECHNIQUE*

Do the Abundance Ritual technique described in Chapter Ten of *The Map to Abundance.* Then, write about your experience using the prompts below.

How did you feel before the technique?

How did you feel afterward?

What changes did you see in your reality as a result of the technique?

Purchase this technique as a meditation at www.LiveALifeYouLove.com!

Abundance Action 6

THE "LOVING MONEY LEAVING"
TECHNIQUE

Do the Loving Money Leaving technique described in Chapter Ten of *The Map to Abundance.* Then, write about your experience using the prompts below.

How did you feel before the technique?

How did you feel afterward?

What changes did you see in your reality as a result of the technique?

Abundance Action 7

Out of all the techniques you tried, which felt most fun and powerful for you, and why? Describing the feelings you created while using your favorite technique will help you create more of the same in the future!

CHAPTER ELEVEN

Action: Bring Your Commitment
Into the World

*A*ction is a requirement in order to manifest abundance. Taking action tells the universe, "I am getting ready, because this kick-ass dream of abundance is about to materialize!" Action is a super-strong message that you believe in your dream, and truly expect it to happen.

Keeping your dreams of abundance in your head without taking action is like setting up a storefront but never unlocking the front door. It's getting 90 percent of the way there, but never actually bringing it into the world so that you can reap the rewards.

However, not just any action will do. Acting for the sake of action—aka doing "busy work"—won't result in attracting abundance. Your actions must be *inspired*.

This chapter is all about identifying inspired action—and then actually doing it!

Abundance Action 1

When you think about your dream of abundance, do you find yourself getting excited?

When you think about taking action toward your dream of abundance, do you feel inspired to take action?

Do you have any hesitancy toward taking action? If so, can you trace it back to the beliefs or the wrong dream that might be causing it?

Abundance Action 2

Make a list of your big dreams, and the inspired actions you'll take to manifest them in the next 30 days. Be sure to check your actions off the list when you've accomplished them!

DREAM #1 _____

INSPIRED ACTIONS   COMPLETED

1. _____   _____

2. _____   _____

3. _____   _____

4. _____   _____

5. _____   _____

6. _____   _____

7. _____   _____

8. _____   _____

9. _____   _____

10. _____   _____

You don't need to have 10 inspired actions for every dream right away—just write down (and do!) as many as feel right for you, and add more as they come to you!

THE MAP TO ABUNDANCE WORKBOOK

DREAM #2 _____

INSPIRED ACTIONS   COMPLETED

1. _____   _____

2. _____   _____

3. _____   _____

4. _____   _____

5. _____   _____

6. _____   _____

7. _____   _____

8. _____   _____

9. _____   _____

10. _____   _____

NOTES

DREAM #3 _____

INSPIRED ACTIONS   COMPLETED

1. _____   _____

2. _____   _____

3. _____   _____

4. _____   _____

5. _____   _____

6. _____   _____

7. _____   _____

8. _____   _____

9. _____   _____

10. _____   _____

NOTES

{extra writing space}

CHAPTER TWELVE

See the "Signs" & Make Them Grow

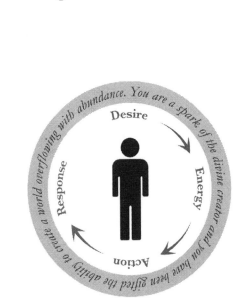

*T*he universe always responds. Everything you see, hear, touch, taste, and experience "out there" is mirroring the thoughts, feelings, and beliefs inside of you.

As you shift and change, your reality will too—but not necessarily all at once. It will likely happen slowly, and you'll receive "signs" to indicate that it is, indeed, changing.

Signs are indications of impending movement. You can see signs of change for just about everything on the planet. Signs occur before relationships change, children change, jobs change, and realities change. If you learn to pay attention to those signs, they can tell you whether you're on track or not—and with that information, you will become more empowered.

Abundance Action 1

Track your progress toward your dreams! Below, write down your big dreams (likely the same ones you worked with in the previous chapter). Then, do one of the techniques from Chapter Ten, and keep track of the signs you receive!

DREAM #1 _____

TECHNIQUE? _____

SIGNS RECEIVED?   DATE

1. _____   _____

2. _____   _____

3. _____   _____

OTHER OBSERVATIONS?

DREAM #2 _____

TECHNIQUE? _____

SIGNS RECEIVED?   DATE

    1. _____   _____

    2. _____   _____

    3. _____   _____

OTHER OBSERVATIONS?

THE MAP TO ABUNDANCE WORKBOOK

DREAM #3 _____

TECHNIQUE? _____

SIGNS RECEIVED?   DATE

1. _____   _____

2. _____   _____

3. _____   _____

OTHER OBSERVATIONS?

Abundance Action 2

Use the applied kinesiology techniques in Appendix B to test for the constricting beliefs discussed throughout Chapter Twelve of *The Map to Abundance*. Document the beliefs that need to be changed, and change them using a technique in Appendix D.

BELIEFS TO CHANGE

1. _____

2. _____

3. _____

4. _____

5. _____

6. _____

7. _____

8. _____

9. _____

10. _____

{extra writing space}

CHAPTER THIRTEEN

Meanwhile, As You Wait for Your Abundance ...

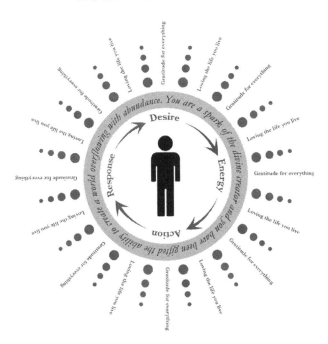

Instead of waiting by the door and driving yourself crazy while you wait for abundance, just have a blast living life!

You see, most people have it backwards. They think you need to create a wonderful job, money, opportunities, etc. in order to have an abundant life.

But, you see, you already have an abundant life. You just haven't realized it, or begun to enjoy it yet.

You have a life in which you are a god. You literally create your world. That, my friend, is the epitome of abundance. If you are creating it all (and you are), you can create unlimited abundance.

Once you let that in, and you begin to enjoy—and I mean really enjoy—every single minute of your life, the stuff you want comes automatically. **Stuff is a side effect of living your abundant life, not a condition for it.**

Abundance Action 1

What makes you happy? Below, make a list of everything in your life that makes you happy. Refer to it every time you start to feel impatient, anxious, sad, or afraid.

• •● MY HAPPY LIST ●• •

1. _____

2. _____

3. _____

4. _____

5. _____

6. _____

7. _____

8. _____

9. _____

10. _____

Get creative with your Happy List! Write out your list on a poster-sized paper and hang it where you will see it every day. Add artwork, photos, and other visual elements to make it really stunning!

Abundance Action 2

Every hour, check your emotional state. (To remind yourself to do this, tie a ribbon around your wrist or set an alarm.) Use this sheet for your first day, then photocopy it or create a sheet in your journal for subsequent days.

••● MY EMOTIONAL STATE ●••

8:00 AM _____

9:00 AM _____

10:00 AM _____

11:00 AM _____

12:00 PM _____

1:00 PM _____

2:00 PM _____

3:00 PM _____

4:00 PM _____

5:00 PM _____

6:00 PM _____

7:00 PM _____

8:00 PM _____

9:00 PM _____

If you're less than happy during your hourly check, ask your higher self to help by saying something like, "Higher self, please help me to shift into the emotion of happiness." Then, make the choice to be happy!

Abundance Action 3

Every day for the next five days, set a timer for 5 minutes and write down everything you're grateful for. (Use the space provided below, or start a gratitude journal!)

••● DAY 1 GRATITUDES ●••

●●● DAY 2 GRATITUDES ●●●

DAY 3 GRATITUDES

••• DAY 4 GRATITUDES •••

DAY 5 GRATITUDES

Abundance Action 4

Use the applied kinesiology techniques in Appendix B to test for the constricting beliefs discussed throughout Chapter Thirteen of *The Map to Abundance*. Document the beliefs that need to be changed, and change them using a technique in Appendix D.

BELIEFS TO CHANGE

1. _____

2. _____

3. _____

4. _____

5. _____

6. _____

7. _____

8. _____

9. _____

10. _____

{extra writing space}

CHAPTER FOURTEEN

Meet Your Financial Partners
(aka Your Unseen Friends)

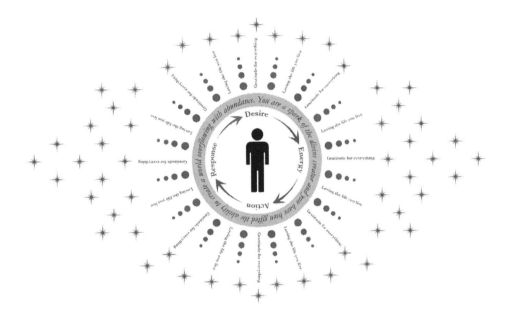

*Y*ou don't have to create your abundance alone.

You can ask for help. You can learn from books (like this one), teachers, friends, and colleagues. You can also receive help from your unseen friends.

Unseen friends are those to whom you are connected on "the other side." They can override the rules of conscious creation on this planet and instantly "gift" you with a reality. They can drop ideas into your mind, place a book or a teacher in your path, or lift an energy that has been keeping you bogged down. They can help you in unlimited ways, but they won't do it for you. You have to participate.

God (and Goddess) gave you life, but they know you want to figure this out yourself, and they won't take that opportunity from you no matter how you beg them. But they *will* help, and so will your other unseen friends.

Abundance Action 1

What (besides creating a life you love) do you think you might be here on Earth to do? Write your thoughts in the space below.

•• ● WHY I'M HERE ● ••

What are your unique talents, strengths, and gifts?

How might you incorporate this destiny with creating/allowing abundance?

Abundance Action 2

Every night and every morning for the next 5 days, ask your unseen friends for something important to you. During this time you've set aside for "asking," make note of the signs you've received from them in response to your request.

• • ● DAY 1 ● • •

WHAT I ASKED FOR _____

_____

SIGNS RECEIVED?

1. _____

2. _____

3. _____

OTHER OBSERVATIONS?

••● DAY 2 ●••

WHAT I ASKED FOR _____

_____

SIGNS RECEIVED?

1. _____

2. _____

3. _____

OTHER OBSERVATIONS?

• •● DAY 3 ●● •

WHAT I ASKED FOR _____

_____

SIGNS RECEIVED?

   1. _____

   2. _____

   3. _____

OTHER OBSERVATIONS?

●●● DAY 4 ●●●

WHAT I ASKED FOR _____

_____

SIGNS RECEIVED?

1. _____

2. _____

3. _____

OTHER OBSERVATIONS?

• • ● DAY 5 ● • •

WHAT I ASKED FOR _____

_____

SIGNS RECEIVED?

1. _____

2. _____

3. _____

OTHER OBSERVATIONS?

Abundance Action 3

Are you willing to get to know your unseen friends better? Set aside 30 minutes this week to meet meditatively with (at least) your higher self, one male guide, and one female guide. Write about your experience below.

••● MY MEDITATIVE EXPERIENCE ●●•

{extra writing space}

CHAPTER FIFTEEN

Abundance Trip-Ups

Money is the hardest thing you'll ever consciously create, and money is the easiest thing you'll ever consciously create.

Why?

We start off with so many limiting beliefs and stumbling blocks around money that creating it will seem illusive and impossible—right up until we change the most limiting beliefs and kick each of those blocks out of the way. Once we create a clear path to the abundance we deserve, though, money will suddenly become the easiest thing we've ever created.

You create your reality. Period. No matter what anyone does around you, says around you, or thinks around you, *you* create your own reality. You are creating your abundance (including but not limited to money) no matter where that abundance comes from.

Abundance Action 1

Who in your life have you allowed to impact you in a negative way. Write out how you'll handle the situation for each person the next time you're tempted to lower your resonance.

NAME _____

HOW I INTEND TO RESPOND

_____

_____

NAME _____

HOW I INTEND TO RESPOND

_____

_____

NAME _____

HOW I INTEND TO RESPOND

_____

_____

Abundance Action 2

Who do you compare yourself to? Can you shift your thinking and become excited that you could have what they have? If not, do some detective work and change those beliefs!

BELIEFS TO CHANGE

1. _____

2. _____

3. _____

Abundance Action 3

Are you afraid of success? Make a list of your fears (and the related beliefs) around success, and change them.

FEAR _____

BELIEF _____

FEAR _____

BELIEF _____

FEAR _____

BELIEF _____

FEAR _____

BELIEF _____

Abundance Action 4

Do the Personifying Success Meditation on page 374 of *The Map to Abundance.* Write about your experience below.

••● MY EXPERIENCE ●●•

Abundance Action 5

Do you share money or resources with another? Have you been unclear about who creates that wealth? Write about the way you've held it in the past, and how you intend to think of it in the future.

Abundance Action 6

Use the applied kinesiology techniques in Appendix B to test for the constricting beliefs discussed throughout Chapter Fifteen of *The Map to Abundance*. Document the beliefs that need to be changed, and change them using a technique in Appendix D.

BELIEFS TO CHANGE

1. _____

2. _____

3. _____

4. _____

5. _____

6. _____

7. _____

8. _____

9. _____

10. _____

{extra writing space}

CHAPTER SIXTEEN

Keeping the Abundance You Create

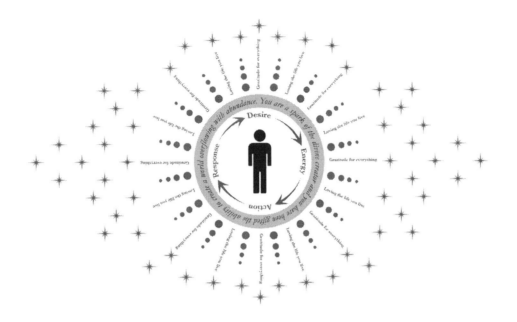

If you don't adjust to wealth—to having it, to accepting it as a way of life, to seeing yourself as wealthy, you will un-create that wealth.

Because we see ourselves in a certain way around money, when we slip out of our comfort zone, we feel awkward and unfamiliar, as if we don't quite belong there.

When our reality shifts to a new reality, our self-image must shift also, or our reality will snap back to the old one. That's why lottery winners lose their millions. It's why many people can't sustain good fortune of any type. It's why some create misfortune after every win. And it's why we find ourselves slipping back into old patterns, time and time again.

Abundance Action 1

What is your current self-image around money? How do you relate to it? What do you do when you have it? What do you do when you don't have it? How does it make you feel?

Write your current self-image statement in the space below. Get as detailed as possible so you can change what isn't working!

● ● ● MY CURRENT SELF-IMAGE ● ● ●

Abundance Action 2

What is your new self-image around money? How do you relate to it? What do you do when you have it? What do you do when you don't have it? How does it make you feel?

Write your new, upgraded self-image statement in the space below. Get as detailed as possible!

• • ● MY UPGRADED SELF-IMAGE ● • •

Abundance Action 3

Write about exactly how you intend to commit to each of the Four Steps to Sustaining the Essence of Abundance.

STEP 1: MAKE TIME FOR CONSCIOUS CREATING EVERY SINGLE DAY.

MY INTENTIONS FOR WORKING WITH CONSCIOUS CREATION DAILY:

STEP 2: MAKE CONSCIOUSLY CREATING ABUNDANCE MY TOP PRIORITY

MY INTENTIONS FOR PRIORITIZING CONSCIOUS CREATION DAILY:

STEP 3: CHECK IN REGULARLY

MY INTENTIONS FOR CHECKING IN AND KEEPING MYSELF ACCOUNTABLE:

STEP 4: STOP THINKING ABOUT IT!

MY INTENTIONS FOR STAYING PRESENT AND GRATEFUL IN THE MOMENT:

{extra writing space}

CHAPTER SEVENTEEN

The Most Important Thing to Remember

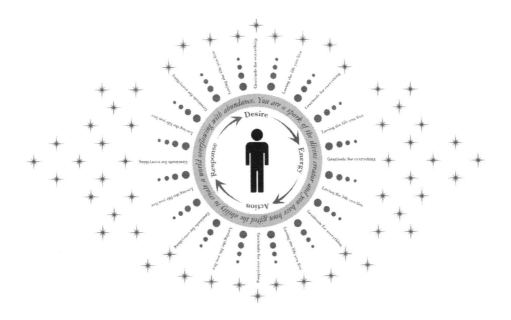

If you come away knowing one concept from this book, I hope it's this: **The easiest way to create abundance (once you believe it's possible) is to forget about making money and focus on living a spectacular life.**

I'm not asking you to forget about making money. Just don't focus on it. Instead, focus on the joy of your life.

If you are living your life with great joy, abandon, excitement, and passion, who the heck cares if it takes a while to be fully and totally abundant? You're having fun! Fun is the point. Joy is the point. Excitement is the point.

Money is not the point.

Money is a side effect of feeling joyously, passionately, beautifully, abundantly in love with your life.

And you can feel that way *now*.

Abundance Action 1

What will your life be like when you have unlimited abundance?
Write about how your daily life will look once you have the
abundance you've been dreaming about.

• •● MY AMAZINGLY ABUNDANT LIFE ●● •

Abundance Action 2

What will your life look like when you are living a life you love and every day is filled with ease, elegance, love, joy, peace, excitement, passion, creativity, and fun?

• • ● MY EXCITING, JOY-FILLED LIFE ● • •

Abundance Action 3

List five ways that you can start living the life you described in Abundance Actions 1 and 2 *right now*.

WHAT I WANT: _____

HOW I CAN HAVE IT NOW:

WHAT I WANT: _____

HOW I CAN HAVE IT NOW:

WHAT I WANT: _____

HOW I CAN HAVE IT NOW:

WHAT I WANT: _____

HOW I CAN HAVE IT NOW:

WHAT I WANT: _____

HOW I CAN HAVE IT NOW:

Abundance Action 4

What do you think your soul and higher self want for you? What can you be doing for your highest good, that is in alignment with your destiny? Write about that.

• • •   WHAT MY SOUL WANTS FOR ME   • • •

CHAPTER EIGHTEEN

Your Plan for Creating Abundance

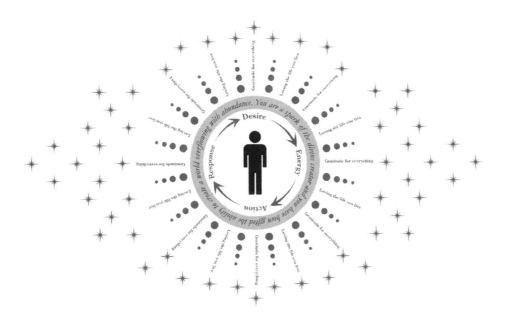

*A*bundance is your birthright.

As a divine being on this planet, you not only deserve abundance, it's built in to your very being. You only need look at nature to recognize that fact.

However, because you are so powerful, you can also create lack, struggle, and hardship. It really is up to you. **If you are committed to creating abundance, and you honestly do the work, you will succeed.**

If my approach works for you, great. If another approach works for you, or if you want to tailor my approach to suit your temperament, that's great too. Trust yourself.

Regardless of the path you choose, I do suggest setting a regular schedule to work on expanding your abundance. When there are thousands of possible directions your mind can be pulled in each day, it's too easy to let this work fall by the wayside. Honor and love yourself enough to make this work a priority in your life.

You will use the space in this chapter to record your Abundance Sessions from Chapter 18 of *The Map To Abundance*.

BEFORE YOU BEGIN THE WORK
IN THIS CHAPTER ...

- Reread any chapters or sections of *The Map to Abundance* that felt particularly powerful to you, and complete the corresponding exercises in this workbook (if you haven't already done so).
- Write your intentions in Chapter 5 of this workbook (or in a separate notebook) and date them. Each time you update your intentions from now on, create a new copy with the current date. This will help you track your progress.

Abundance Session 1

STEP 1

Find a quiet place to be alone. Turn off your phone and internet. If you like, light a candle and play some soft music. Find your center, and relax.

STEP 2

Call upon your unseen friends to guide and assist you during this session. Say something like:

> *Higher self, soul, counselors, angels, and other beings of love and light, help me to create an abundant life. Assist me in recognizing the beliefs, patterns, thoughts, and feelings that limit my abundance, and help me to change what stands in my way. Thank you.*

STEP 3

Pretend that you have stepped five or ten years into the future. Read your abundance intentions, feeling and knowing that every single one of them has come true. Think about how much your life has changed since you wrote them.

Write your observations and gratitudes in the space below:

STEP 4

If you have any beliefs from previous chapters that you tested for (or otherwise know are yours) that you haven't changed, change up to ten beliefs now.

BELIEFS TO CHANGE

1. _____

2. _____

3. _____

4. _____

5. _____

6. _____

7. _____

8. _____

9. _____

10. _____

STEP 5

Do the One-Minute Manifestor Technique from Chapter Ten for one of your intentions of abundance. Write your observations and any signs you receive over the next several days in the space below.

THE MAP TO ABUNDANCE WORKBOOK

STEP 6

Revisit Chapter Six. Of the Abundance Stoppers listed in that chapter (fear, doubt, victimhood, self-pity, entitlement, envy, and guilt) which presents the biggest challenge for you? Write about your pattern of allowing this Abundance Stopper, and how you will handle it the next time it rears its ugly head.

STEP 7

Find support in your newly-created, abundant reality. Who can you turn to with questions, ideas, excitement for all of the new abundances manifesting and any challenges that may come up along the way? List everyone you know who can help you in the space below.

MY ABUNDANCE HELPERS

1. _____

2. _____

3. _____

4. _____

5. _____

6. _____

If you don't have people in your life right now to support you, find fellow creators at www. LiveALifeYouLove. com/support.

STEP 8

Thank your unseen friends for the assistance they've given you throughout this session, and for the ongoing assistance they will provide. Say something like:

Higher self, soul, counselors, angels, and other beings of love and light, thank you for helping me to create an abundant life. Please continue to assist me in recognizing the beliefs, patterns, thoughts, and feelings that limit my abundance, and continue to help me to change what stands in my way. Thank you.

•• ● NOTES ● ••

Abundance Session 2

STEP 1

Find a quiet place to be alone. Turn off your phone and internet. If you like, light a candle and play some soft music. Find your center, and relax.

STEP 2

Call upon your unseen friends to guide and assist you during this session. Say something like:

> Higher self, soul, counselors, angels, and other beings of love and light, help me to create an abundant life. Assist me in recognizing the beliefs, patterns, thoughts, and feelings that limit my abundance, and help me to change what stands in my way. Thank you.

STEP 3

Read your Commitment to Abundance (from Chapter Three). Recommit yourself to your abundance and the work you will do to create it.

STEP 4

Visit your child and adolescent selves in meditation. (Ask your higher self to take you to the child self or adolescent self that is most appropriate.) Allow your child and adolescent to fully express their fear, disappointment, guilt, and/or any other emotion around money. Give your child and adolescent selves a money machine (even if you have given them one before). Ask them what they plan to use the money for. Encourage them to spend the money freely, because there is always more where that came from.

Make a note to visit them in meditation again the following day to see how they spent the money. Be excited for them, and for yourself! The more easily money flows for your child and adolescent selves, the more easily money will flow for you.

STEP 5

If you have any beliefs from previous chapters that you tested for (or otherwise know are yours) that you haven't changed, change up to ten beliefs now.

BELIEFS TO CHANGE

1. _____

2. _____

3. _____

4. _____

5. _____

6. _____

7. _____

8. _____

9. _____

10. _____

STEP 6

Do the One-Minute Manifestor Technique from Chapter Ten for one of your intentions of abundance. Write your observations and any signs you receive over the next several days in the space below.

STEP 7

Make note of any signs of abundance you have received.

SIGNS I'VE RECEIVED

1. _____

2. _____

3. _____

4. _____

5. _____

6. _____

7. _____

8. _____

9. _____

10. _____

If you can't remember or haven't noticed, revisit Chapter Twelve to remind yourself how a sign might show up. Then set a reminder every day to think about the signs you may have received, and record them.

STEP 8

Thank your unseen friends for the assistance they've given you throughout this session, and for the ongoing assistance they will provide. Say something like:

Higher self, soul, counselors, angels, and other beings of love and light, thank you for helping me to create an abundant life. Please continue to assist me in recognizing the beliefs, patterns, thoughts, and feelings that limit my abundance, and continue to help me to change what stands in my way. Thank you.

•••● NOTES ●•••

Abundance Session 3

STEP 1

Find a quiet place to be alone. Turn off your phone and internet. If you like, light a candle and play some soft music. Find your center, and relax.

STEP 2

Call upon your unseen friends to guide and assist you during this session. Say something like:

> *Higher self, soul, counselors, angels, and other beings of love and light, help me to create an abundant life. Assist me in recognizing the beliefs, patterns, thoughts, and feelings that limit my abundance, and help me to change what stands in my way. Thank you.*

STEP 3

Do the One-Minute Manifestor Technique from Chapter Ten for one of your intentions of abundance. Write your observations and any signs you receive over the next several days in the space below.

STEP 4

Talk to your negative self about your dreams of manifesting money and other forms of abundance. What does it say in response? Write that down, and determine if there are any underlying beliefs associated with your negative self's statements. If so, change them in the next step.

WHAT MY NEGATIVE SELF HAS TO SAY ...

STEP 5

If you have any beliefs from this or previous chapters that you tested for (or otherwise know are yours) that you haven't changed, change up to ten beliefs now.

BELIEFS TO CHANGE

1. _____

2. _____

3. _____

4. _____

5. _____

6. _____

7. _____

8. _____

9. _____

10. _____

STEP 6

On the next page, make a list of 25 ways your life is already abundant, but which have nothing to do with money. Now, choose to let the abundance you already have spread into your financial life.

I AM ABUNDANT BECAUSE ....

1. _____
2. _____
3. _____
4. _____
5. _____
6. _____
7. _____
8. _____
9. _____
10. _____
11. _____
12. _____
13. _____
14. _____
15. _____
16. _____
17. _____
18. _____
19. _____
20. _____
21. _____
22. _____
23. _____
24. _____
25. _____

STEP 7

Do the Abundant Future Self Technique from Chapter Ten. Write about your experience below, including any signs you receive over the next several days.

STEP 8

Thank your unseen friends for the assistance they've given you throughout this session, and for the ongoing assistance they will provide. Say something like:

> *Higher self, soul, counselors, angels, and other beings of love and light, thank you for helping me to create an abundant life. Please continue to assist me in recognizing the beliefs, patterns, thoughts, and feelings that limit my abundance, and continue to help me to change what stands in my way. Thank you.*

•••● NOTES ●•••

Abundance Session 4

STEP 1

Find a quiet place to be alone. Turn off your phone and internet. If you like, light a candle and play some soft music. Find your center, and relax.

STEP 2

Call upon your unseen friends to guide and assist you during this session. Say something like:

> *Higher self, soul, counselors, angels, and other beings of love and light, help me to create an abundant life. Assist me in recognizing the beliefs, patterns, thoughts, and feelings that limit my abundance, and help me to change what stands in my way. Thank you.*

STEP 3

Do the One-Minute Manifestor Technique from Chapter Ten for one of your intentions of abundance. Write your observations and any signs you receive over the next several days in the space below.

STEP 4

If you have any beliefs from this or previous chapters that you tested for (or otherwise know are yours) that you haven't changed, change up to ten beliefs now.

BELIEFS TO CHANGE

1. _____

2. _____

3. _____

4. _____

5. _____

6. _____

7. _____

8. _____

9. _____

10. _____

STEP 5

Make note of any signs of abundance you have received since your last Abundance Session.

SIGNS I'VE RECEIVED

1. _____

2. _____

3. _____

4. _____

5. _____

6. _____

7. _____

8. _____

9. _____

10. _____

STEP 6

When you think about who you are in relation to abundance and money, what do you come up with? Do you automatically think, "I am truly abundant. Money comes to me easily and elegantly. I will never have an issue with money again," or something like that?

If not, do the image work on the next page (which is also detailed in Chapter Sixteen of *The Map to Abundance*).

Write a paragraph about the image you currently have around money in your life.

Now, write a paragraph about the image you would prefer to have around money.

Do the image-shifting meditation described on page 388 of *The Map to Abundance*. Write about your experience below.

STEP 7

Thought Police: What thoughts do you continually have (especially around money)? There's no need to catch every thought; simply take your emotional temperature every hour, on the hour, for the next 24 hours. Anytime you don't feel fabulous, ask yourself why. Trace the feelings back to your thoughts. Investigate the underlying beliefs, then change them.

Thought _____

Belief _____

Changed?   Y N

Thought _____

Belief _____

Changed?   Y N

Thought _____

Belief _____

Changed?   Y   N

Thought _____

Belief _____

Changed?   Y   N

STEP 8

Thank your unseen friends for the assistance they've given you throughout this session, and for the ongoing assistance they will provide. Say something like:

> *Higher self, soul, counselors, angels, and other beings of love and light, thank you for helping me to create an abundant life. Please continue to assist me in recognizing the beliefs, patterns, thoughts, and feelings that limit my abundance, and continue to help me to change what stands in my way. Thank you.*

Abundance Session 5

STEP 1

Find a quiet place to be alone. Turn off your phone and internet. If you like, light a candle and play some soft music. Find your center, and relax.

STEP 2

Call upon your unseen friends to guide and assist you during this session. Say something like:

> *Higher self, soul, counselors, angels, and other beings of love and light, help me to create an abundant life. Assist me in recognizing the beliefs, patterns, thoughts, and feelings that limit my abundance, and help me to change what stands in my way. Thank you.*

STEP 3

Do the One-Minute Manifestor Technique from Chapter Ten for one of your intentions of abundance. Write your observations and any signs you receive over the next several days in the space below.

STEP 4

If you have any beliefs from this or previous chapters that you tested for (or otherwise know are yours) that you haven't changed, change up to ten beliefs now.

BELIEFS TO CHANGE

1. _____

2. _____

3. _____

4. _____

5. _____

6. _____

7. _____

8. _____

9. _____

10. _____

STEP 5

Revisit Chapter Eight and make a list of the Dad and authority figures you had as a child/adolescent. Visit with each of them in meditation and tell them how you felt—the good and the bad. Allow that expression of emotion to heal them, and any issues with abundance.

MY FATHER/AUTHORITY FIGURES

Name _____

What I learned in meditation:

Name _____

What I learned in meditation:

Name _____

What I learned in meditation:

THE MAP TO ABUNDANCE WORKBOOK

STEP 6

Make note of any signs of abundance you have received since your last Abundance Session.

SIGNS I'VE RECEIVED

1. _____
2. _____
3. _____
4. _____
5. _____
6. _____
7. _____
8. _____
9. _____
10. _____

STEP 7

Do you love your life? What can you do right now to love it even more?

Spend 30-60 minutes doing something you absolutely adore, or schedule the time to do that within the next 72 hours.

WHAT I'M GOING TO DO:

STEP 8

Reality Check: How are you doing with the Four Steps to Sustaining the Essence of Abundance?

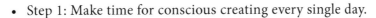

- Step 1: Make time for conscious creating every single day.

- Step 2: Make consciously creating abundance my top priority.

- Step 3: Check in regularly.

- Step 4: Stop thinking about it!

Write about your experience with the Four Steps below.

STEP 9

Thank your unseen friends for the assistance they've given you throughout this session, and for the ongoing assistance they will provide. Say something like:

Higher self, soul, counselors, angels, and other beings of love and light, thank you for helping me to create an abundant life. Please continue to assist me in recognizing the beliefs, patterns, thoughts, and feelings that limit my abundance, and continue to help me to change what stands in my way. Thank you.

• • ● NOTES ● ● •

Abundance Session 6

STEP 1

Find a quiet place to be alone. Turn off your phone and internet. If you like, light a candle and play some soft music. Find your center, and relax.

STEP 2

Call upon your unseen friends to guide and assist you during this session. Say something like:

> *Higher self, soul, counselors, angels, and other beings of love and light, help me to create an abundant life. Assist me in recognizing the beliefs, patterns, thoughts, and feelings that limit my abundance, and help me to change what stands in my way. Thank you.*

STEP 3

Do the One-Minute Manifestor Technique from Chapter Ten for one of your intentions of abundance. Write your observations and any signs you receive over the next several days in the space below.

STEP 4

If you have any beliefs from this or previous chapters that you tested for (or otherwise know are yours) that you haven't changed, change up to ten beliefs now.

BELIEFS TO CHANGE

1. _____

2. _____

3. _____

4. _____

5. _____

6. _____

7. _____

8. _____

9. _____

10. _____

THE MAP TO ABUNDANCE WORKBOOK

STEP 5

Write about what your life will be like when money is no longer an issue. What will you do differently? What choices will you make?

STEP 6

In meditation, visit the younger adult selves who had the most challenges regarding money and abundance. Assuming you worked with them at the end of Chapter Seven, go back and find out how their lives have changed since you gave them a reality where all their dreams came true. (If you haven't done that work, do it now. Then, revisit your younger adult selves in a day or so.)

MY YOUNGER SELVES

Name _____

Changes I observed:

Name _____

Changes I observed:

Name _____

Changes I observed:

Name _____

Changes I observed:

STEP 7

On a scale of 1 to 10, how happy do you stay throughout your days?

        1   2   3   4   5   6   7   8   9   10

If less than a ten out of ten, how could you be happier? (If you're not sure, you may want to revisit Chapter Thirteen.)

STEP 8

Make note of any signs of abundance you have received since your last Abundance Session.

SIGNS I'VE RECEIVED

1. _____

2. _____

3. _____

4. _____

5. _____

6. _____

7. _____

STEP 9

Thank your unseen friends for the assistance they've given you throughout this session, and for the ongoing assistance they will provide. Say something like:

Higher self, soul, counselors, angels, and other beings of love and light, thank you for helping me to create an abundant life. Please continue to assist me in recognizing the beliefs, patterns, thoughts, and feelings that limit my abundance, and continue to help me to change what stands in my way. Thank you.

•●● NOTES ●●•

Abundance Session 7

STEP 1

Find a quiet place to be alone. Turn off your phone and internet. If you like, light a candle and play some soft music. Find your center, and relax.

STEP 2

Call upon your unseen friends to guide and assist you during this session. Say something like:

> *Higher self, soul, counselors, angels, and other beings of love and light, help me to create an abundant life. Assist me in recognizing the beliefs, patterns, thoughts, and feelings that limit my abundance, and help me to change what stands in my way. Thank you.*

STEP 3

Do the One-Minute Manifestor Technique from Chapter Ten for one of your intentions of abundance. Write your observations and any signs you receive over the next several days in the space below.

STEP 4

If you have any beliefs from this or previous chapters that you tested for (or otherwise know are yours) that you haven't changed, change up to ten beliefs now.

BELIEFS TO CHANGE

1. _____

2. _____

3. _____

4. _____

5. _____

6. _____

7. _____

8. _____

9. _____

10. _____

STEP 5

Go shopping (in a store or online). While you shop, do the I Can Afford Everything Here Technique. Write about the experience below.

STEP 6

Meditate with your future self—the one who is most abundant and happy. Ask for his or her advice in maintaining an abundant resonance. Write about what you learned below.

STEP 7

How grateful are you? Do you count your blessings hourly? Daily? Weekly? Less often? Make a list of twenty-five things you are grateful for (including monetary items).

I AM GRATEFUL FOR ...

1. _____
2. _____
3. _____
4. _____
5. _____
6. _____
7. _____
8. _____
9. _____
10. _____
11. _____
12. _____
13. _____
14. _____
15. _____
16. _____
17. _____
18. _____
19. _____
20. _____

21. _____

22. _____

23. _____

24. _____

25. _____

STEP 8

Make note of any signs of abundance you have received since your last Abundance Session.

SIGNS I'VE RECEIVED

1. _____

2. _____

3. _____

4. _____

5. _____

6. _____

STEP 9

Thank your unseen friends for the assistance they've given you throughout this session, and for the ongoing assistance they will provide. Say something like:

> *Higher self, soul, counselors, angels, and other beings of love and light, thank you for helping me to create an abundant life. Please continue to assist me in recognizing the beliefs, patterns, thoughts, and feelings that limit my abundance, and continue to help me to change what stands in my way. Thank you.*

••● NOTES ●••

AFTERWORD

I'm Grateful for You

It is my greatest joy to teach others about conscious creation, and get the word out about how this whole creation thing actually works. I know how exciting it is to watch your life change right before your eyes, as if by magic—and the next most exciting thing is watching others' lives change as they work the same magic.

Thank you for reading, my fellow creator. I wish you all the abundance in the world. It's there, just waiting for you to allow it in.

If you enjoyed this book or it proves useful to you, I'd be most grateful if you would let me know.

I'd truly appreciate it if you'd review this book on Amazon, Barnes & Noble, or wherever you purchased it. Reviews do matter to an author—I read them all!—and to readers. It would be a great honor for me to receive a review from you.

If you'd like to reach me personally, e-mail me at BoniLonnsburry@ LiveALifeYouLove.com.

With all my love,

Boni

PS: Sharing your successes not only improves your ability to create (because by sharing it you make it more real), it inspires others and fills them with hope to create their own successes. Share your creations at www.LiveALifeYouLove.com/inspire.

RESOURCES

Learn More About Conscious Creation

ON THE WEB

To purchase other books by Boni, guided meditations mentioned in this book, and Success and Creation Journals, visit www.LiveALifeYouLove.com/shop.

Learn more about Boni's twelve-week training program and other courses at www.CreationSchool.com.

SOCIAL MEDIA

Facebook: www.facebook.com/LivealifeyoulovewithBoniLonnsburry

Private Facebook group:
www.Facebook.com/groups/consciouslycreatingalifeyoulove

Twitter: @BoniLonnsburry

YouTube: www.YouTube.com/user/BoniLonnsburry

OTHER

To learn more about Lazaris, visit www.Lazaris.com.

ABOUT *the* AUTHOR

Boni Lonnsburry

*B*oni Lonnsburry is the Chief Visionary Officer of Inner Art Inc., an expert on conscious creation, and the author of four books, including *The Map to Abundance: The No-Exceptions Guide to Creating Money. Success, & Bliss,* which has won multiple awards including two CIPA awards, three Indie Excellence Awards, and the Silver Benjamin Franklin Award, and was a finalist in two categories in the Next Generation Indies Awards.

Her first best-selling book, *The Map: To Our Responsive Universe, Where Dreams Really Do Come True!,* has won eight book awards, including the prestigious Nautilus Award, and was named "Best Law of Attraction Book of 2013" by Law of Attraction Leaders.

By applying the Universal Law of Attraction, Boni transformed her life of poverty, loneliness, and despair to one of abundance, love, and joy. She now teaches others to do the same.

Learn more about Boni at www.LiveALifeYouLove.com and www.CreationSchool.com.

More Award-Winning Books
by Boni Lonnsburry

The Map to Abundance: The No-Exceptions Guide to Creating Money, Success, & Bliss (2017)

The Map: To Our Responsive Universe, Where Dreams Really Do Come True! (2013)

The Map Workbook (2015)

Messages from Your Unseen Friends: Volume I (2015)

Messages from Your Unseen Friends: Volume II (2018)

Life on Planet Earth: A User's Guide (e-book)